Editor
Eric Migliaccio

Managing Editor
Ina Massler Levin, M.A.

Editor-in-Chief
Sharon Coan, M.S. Ed.

Cover Artist
Barb Lorseyedi

Art Coordinator
Kevin Barnes

Imaging
Alfred Lau
James Edward Grace

Product Manager
Phil Garcia

Publisher
Mary D. Smith, M.S. Ed.

Grammar, Usage & Mechanics

Practice Makes Perfect

GRADE 3

Authors

Melissa Hart, M.F.A.

Teacher Created Resources, Inc.
6421 Industry Way
Westminster, CA 92683
www.teachercreated.com
ISBN: 978-0-7439-3346-9
©2002 Teacher Created Resources, Inc.
Reprinted, 2010
Made in U.S.A.

Table of Contents

Introduction

The old adage "practice makes perfect" can really hold true for your child and his or her education. The more practice and exposure your child has with concepts being taught in school, the more success he or she is likely to find. For many parents, knowing how to help their children may be frustrating because the resources may not be readily available.

As a parent, it is also difficult to know where to focus your efforts so that the extra practice your child receives at home supports what he or she is learning in school.

This book has been written to help parents and teachers reinforce basic skills with children. *Practice Makes Perfect: Grammar, Usage, & Mechanics* reviews basic grammar skills for third graders. The exercises in this book can be done sequentially or can be taken out of order, as needed.

The following standards or objectives will be met or reinforced by completing the practice pages included in this book. These standards and objectives are similar to the ones required by your state and school district. These standards and objectives are appropriate for third graders.

- The student uses capitalization appropriately.
- The student uses common and proper nouns.
- The student uses plural, singular, possessive, and collective naming nouns.
- The student uses pronouns and substitutes pronouns for nouns.
- The student uses verbs in written compositions.
- The student uses a wide variety of action verbs.
- The student uses past- and present-tense verbs.
- The student uses descriptive words and adjectives.
- The student uses adverbs to make comparisons.
- The student uses apostrophes and quotation marks properly.
- The student uses conjunctions as connecting words.
- The student uses colons between the hour and the minutes when writing the time.
- The student avoids the use of double negatives.

How to Make the Most of This Book

Here are some useful ideas for making the most of this book:

- Set aside a specific place in your home to work on this book. Keep it neat and tidy, with the necessary materials on hand.
- Set up a certain time of day to work on these practice pages to establish consistency; or look for times in your day or week that are less hectic and more conducive to practicing skills.
- Keep all practice sessions with your child positive and constructive. If your child becomes frustrated or tense, set the book aside and look for another time to practice. Forcing your child to perform will not help. Do not use this book as a punishment.
- Help beginning readers with instructions.
- Review the work your child has done.
- Allow the child to use whatever writing instruments he or she prefers. For example, colored pencils can add variety and pleasure to drill work.
- Pay attention to the areas in which your child has the most difficulty. Provide extra guidance and exercises in those areas.
- Look for ways to make real-life application to the skills being reinforced. Play games with your child, such as looking for nouns or verbs.

Nouns

A *noun* is a person, place, or thing.

Underline the nouns in the sentences below. The first one has been done for you.

1. The <u>girl</u> received a <u>puppy</u> for her <u>birthday</u>.

2. The puppy ran in circles and licked her face.

3. "This puppy is the best present ever!" the girl cried.

4. Together, the girl and the puppy went for a walk in the park.

5. The puppy chased butterflies and squirrels.

6. The girl gave her new puppy some water back at home.

7. "Puppies need a lot of sleep," said her mother.

8. Her mother put a blanket in a basket.

9. The puppy crawled into his new bed and fell asleep.

10. The girl slept on the floor beside her pet.

Proper Nouns

A *proper noun* is the name of a specific person, place, or thing.

Underline the proper nouns in the sentences below. The first one has been done for you.

1. <u>Louisa May Alcott</u> wrote a book titled <u>Little Women</u>.

2. Alcott based Little Women on her family.

3. In the book, there are four sisters named Meg, Jo, Beth, and Amy March.

4. The March sisters live with their mother in a New England town.

5. Father is off fighting in the Civil War.

6. Jo wants to be a writer like her favorite author, Charles Dickens.

7. Amy wants to be an artist, and she travels to France.

8. Beth gets scarlet fever after taking care of a sick family.

9. Meg marries John Brooke, which makes her Aunt March angry.

10. After Little Women was published, Alcott wrote these two sequels: Little Men and Jo's Boys.

Abstract Nouns

An *abstract noun* is the name of something that can be talked about, but can't be seen or touched.

Underline the abstract nouns in the sentences below. The first one has been done for you.

1. <u>Happiness</u> is a difficult <u>emotion</u> to define.

2. Different people get joy from different things.

3. Having fun makes many people glad.

4. Others feel happiness when showing kindness to strangers.

5. A great man once said, "Follow your bliss."

6. He meant that people should have a great love.

7. This passion might be art, music, sports, or religion.

8. You must have courage to pursue your dreams.

9. Freedom is an important part of happiness.

10. People can enjoy success without having wealth.

Collective Nouns

A *collective noun* represents a group of things.

Underline the collective nouns in the sentences below. The first one has been done for you.

1. Our class went to the park for a picnic.

2. We learned about a tribe of Native Americans who used to live on the land.

3. I saw a herd of deer eating grass.

4. My best friend gathered a pound of pinecones in a bag.

5. Our teacher picked a bouquet of flowers.

6. She pointed out a flock of crows in the trees.

7. She brought out a bunch of grapes and a batch of cookies.

8. We sat in a grove of pine trees to eat.

9. Little did we know that we were sitting on an army of ants!

10. One student starting running as if he was being chased by a swarm of bees.

Nouns, Nouns, Everywhere!

Insert nouns into the sentences below. The first one has been done for you.

1. Lily and Cody had a birthday __party_____.

2. Lily's mother decorated the room with _____.

3. Cody's father brought over a _____ so that they could play music.

4. The cake was chocolate with white _____.

5. Everyone played Pin the Tail on the _____.

6. Later, Cody and Lily opened their _____.

7. Cassidy gave Cody a _____.

8. Lily received a _____ from her cousin, Marley.

9. Each _____ got a goody-bag full of candy.

10. Later, Lily's mother and Cody's father cleaned the _____.

Plural Nouns

If a noun is *singular*, it means there is only one. *Plural* nouns indicate more than one.

Change the singular nouns below to plural nouns. Then use each of them in a sentence. The first one has been done for you.

1. snake _____*snakes*_____

2. soda _____

3. goose _____

4. box _____

5. scarf _____

6. potato _____

7. mouse _____

8. child _____

9. woman _____

10. apple _____

1. _My friend Karen is afraid of_
    snakes. _____

2. _____
    _____

3. _____
    _____

4. _____
    _____

5. _____
    _____

6. _____
    _____

7. _____
    _____

8. _____
    _____

9. _____
    _____

10. _____
    _____

Pronouns

Pronouns take the place of nouns.

Underline the pronouns in the sentences below. The first one has been done for you.

1. I like to read about former presidents of the United States.

2. Thomas Jefferson is interesting to me.

3. He wrote the Declaration of Independence.

4. You have to read it in high school.

5. Jefferson and other patriots helped to guarantee freedom for us.

6. We should be thankful to the patriots for their struggles.

7. They worked hard to build a new country.

8. I also admire Abraham Lincoln.

9. He helped to make America strong.

10. We owe a lot to these fine presidents, and if they were alive, I would thank them.

Pronouns *(cont.)*

Rewrite the story, using pronouns to replace the underlined nouns. The first one has been done for you.

1. I went to the parade with Mom, and <u>Mom and I</u> ate cotton candy.   *I went to the parade with Mom, and we ate cotton candy.*

2. <u>The cotton candy</u> left our hands sticky. _____

   _____

3. <u>Mom and I</u> waved at the clowns. _____

   _____

4. The clowns waved back at <u>Mom and me</u>. _____

   _____

5. Drummers passed by, and <u>the drummers</u> beat out a marching tune. _____

   _____

6. <u>Mom and I</u> bought red and blue snow cones. _____

   _____

7. Mom's dripped on <u>Mom's</u> sneakers. _____

   _____

8. I looked at <u>Mom</u> and laughed. _____

   _____

9. "Look at your own shoes," <u>Mom</u> said. _____

   _____

10. I looked at my shoes, and <u>my shoes</u> were spotted blue and red. _____

   _____

Action Verbs

Action verbs describe an action that you can see.

Underline the action verbs in the following sentences. The first one has been done for you.

1. Marie <u>enjoys</u> running.

2. She runs with a group of people every Sunday.

3. One person marks a four-mile trail with flour.

4. The rest of them search for the trail.

5. The runners splash through puddles and leap over fallen logs.

6. They climb over fences and fall in the mud.

7. Finally, they burst through the finish line.

8. Marie and her friends wash their hands and faces.

9. Then they sit in the park and drink water.

10. Later, they eat spaghetti and talk about how much fun they had running that day.

Action Verbs *(cont.)*

Fill in the blanks with action verbs to complete the following sentences. The first one has been done for you.

1. We like to __*visit*_____ the beach.

2. My father always _____ in the ocean.

3. My sister and I _____ sand castles.

4. Mother loves to _____ shells.

5. For lunch, we _____ sandwiches and apple juice.

6. Then we all _____ under the umbrella for an hour.

7. Later, I _____ and _____ in the ocean.

8. Once, I saw a dolphin _____ toward me.

9. When the sun _____ down below the horizon, we _____ our towels.

10. We _____ home and into bed and _____.

Helping Verbs

> **Helping verbs** help other verbs to create verb phrases.

Underline the helping verbs in each sentence. The first one has been done for you.

1. Jonathan <u>is</u> working as a photographer.

2. He has owned three different cameras.

3. He is focusing on nature photography.

4. Last week, he was taking pictures in the woods.

5. Mosquitoes were flying around his head.

6. He snapped a picture of a mosquito that was sitting on his lens.

7. Jonathan is going to develop this photograph today.

8. He will send it to a photography contest.

9. If he wins, he will be happy.

10. With the prize money, he is going to buy another camera.

Helling Verbs *(cont.)*

Fill in the blanks with helping verbs to complete the following sentences. The first one has been done for you.

1. My family _____is_____ taking a summer vacation to Florida this year.

2. We _____ going to visit California, but Mom fears earthquakes.

3. In Florida, we _____ take a boat through the Everglades.

4. Last year, my friend _____ surprised by an amazing sight.

5. He saw an alligator, and it _____ sitting in the gutter.

6. I _____ already started packing for the trip.

7. I _____ take my pencils and my sketchbook.

8. Dad says he _____ pay me for a good sketch of an alligator.

9. We _____ going swimming in the ocean, too.

10. There _____ be beautiful fish that I _____ draw for Dad.

Verb Tenses

Verbs can appear in the *past*, *present*, or *future tense*.

Circle the appropriate verb tense in the sentences below. The first one has been done for you.

1. Yesterday, I (**stepped**, **step**, **will step**) on a nail.

2. It (**went, goes, will go**) right through my shoe.

3. My foot (**swelled, swells, will swell**) up last night.

4. My mother (**washed, washes, will wash**) my foot before I went to bed.

5. Now I (**sat, sit, will sit**) in the doctor's office.

6. He (**walked, walks, will walk**) in and says "Hello!"

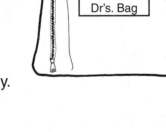

Dr's. Bag

7. I (**needed, need, will need**) a tetanus shot immediately.

8. "Ouch!" I (**cried, cry, will cry**) as the needle enters my hip.

9. The doctor informed me that I (**was, am, will be**) sore tomorrow.

10. I (**watched, watch, will watch**) where I walk in the future.

Subjects and Verbs

> The *subject* of the sentence is the person or thing that performs an action. The verb must agree with the subject.

Rewrite the sentences below to show which verb best agrees with each underlined subject. The first one has been done for you.

1. Marathon runners (**is, are**) usually in very good physical shape.

   Marathon runners are usually in very good physical shape.

2. They (**run, runs**) many miles every week.

   _____

3. A marathon (**is, are**) 26 miles long.

   _____

4. People (**trains, train**) for months to run this challenging race.

   _____

5. Sometimes runners (**come, comes**) over from different countries.

   _____

6. The winner (**get, gets**) a cash prize.

   _____

7. The prize often (**total, totals**) thousands of dollars.

   _____

8. Sometimes runners (**faints, faint**) during a marathon.

   _____

9. Doctors (**stand, stands**) at the sidelines in case someone needs help.

   _____

10. Would you (**attempts, attempt**) such a long race?

    _____

Adjectives

Adjectives are words that describe a noun.

Underline the adjectives in the sentences below. The first one has been done for you.

1. We went to the <u>amazing</u> Museum of Science and Industry.

2. I made a huge dinosaur move by pushing a red button.

3. My friend turned a big wheel to create static electricity.

4. His long, black hair stood straight up on his head!

5. Later, we saw a real human brain.

6. It was suspended in a glass jar full of clear liquid.

7. I learned some interesting information about the history of telephones.

8. We also took a difficult quiz to test our knowledge of gravity.

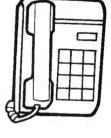

9. My father liked the big, colorful gift shop located in the lobby.

10. He bought a life-sized model of a human heart and plastic stars that glow in the dark.

Adjectives *(cont.)*

Fill in the blanks with adjectives to complete the following sentences. The first one has been done for you.

1. Making cookies is _____ fun _____.

2. First, you have to wash your _____ hands.

3. Then you have to get out a _____
   bowl and mix up your ingredients.

4. Put the cookies in a
   _____ oven.

5. You shouldn't let them bake for a _____ time.

6. The cookies are done when they smell _____.

7. They taste _____ with a glass of milk.

8. I like to bake _____ cookies.

9. I take them in my lunchbox, and all my friends feel _____.

10. Next weekend, I will try to make a _____ cake.

Adverbs

> **Adverbs** describe verbs, adjectives, and other adverbs. Often, an adverb ends in **-ly**.

Underline the adverbs in the sentences below. The first one has been done for you.

1. You can make <u>beautifully</u> decorated masks out of papier mâché.

2. First, carefully blow up a large balloon.

3. Then, gently stir together a mixture of flour and water to make paste.

4. Dip strips of newspaper quickly into the paste.

5. Paste the wet strips smoothly onto the balloon.

6. Cover half of the balloon solidly with several layers of newspaper.

7. Then you should wait patiently for the paste to dry.

8. At last, you can gently pop the balloon.

9. Cautiously cut holes in the mask for eyes and a mouth.

10. Then you can paint your mask brightly and put it on.

Adverbs *(cont.)*

Fill in the blanks with adverbs to complete the following sentences. The first one has been done for you.

1. Tony and Jim like to decorate the house _____*festively*_____ for Christmas.

2. They _____ string cranberries and popcorn to put on their tree.

3. Jim _____ hangs the big wreath above the fireplace.

4. Tony looks _____ at the gingerbread house on the table.

5. Red and green candles are burning _____ everywhere.

6. A wonderful smell comes _____ from the oven.

7. It's Mother's cookies, which she _____ prepared.

8. Everyone stops decorating and _____ gobbles the cookies.

9. Then Jim _____ makes a fire in the fireplace.

10. Everyone sits and _____ admires the decorations.

Expanding Sentences

> **You can use adjectives and adverbs to add detail to your sentences.**

Add an adjective and/or adverb to the sentences below. The first one has been done for you.

1. The _____happy_____ family went camping at Yosemite National Park.
    [adjective]

2. Mother _____ put up the tent while Father built a _____ fire.
    [adverb]   [adjective]

3. I _____ stuck _____ marshmallows on a stick.
    [adverb]   [adjective]

4. I roasted them until they turned _____.
                                      [adjective]

5. Later, we sat around the fire and told _____ stories.
                                            [adjective]

6. Mother yawned _____ and said it was time for bed.
                  [adverb]

7. I crawled into my _____ sleeping bag and fell asleep _____.
                      [adjective]   [adverb]

8. I woke to a _____ sound outside the tent.
                [adjective]

9. "It's a bear!" I called _____.
                            [adverb]

10. "It's just me getting a _____ snack," said Dad _____.
                            [adjective]   [adverb]

Periods

Periods are used at the end of sentences, as well as in initials, abbreviations, and titles before names. Note: A sentence should never end in two periods, even if the last word of the sentence is an abbreviation. (Example: We celebrated the birthday of Dr. Martin Luther King, Jr.)

Add periods where needed in the sentences below. The first one has been done for you.

1. Mr. Munchinmorger's initials are M.M.

2. His full name is Mr Marvin Munchinmorger

3. Marvin Munchinmorger has a wife named Mrs Muchinmorger

4. Her first name is Maude

5. Mrs Maude Munchinmorger's initials are also M M

6. The Munchinmorgers live in Jackson, Miss , on a farm

7. Their cousins, the Dangledoors, live in Washington, D C , in an apartment

8. The Dangledoors live in Apt #5

9. Ms Dangledoor likes to visit Maude Munchinmorger in Mississippi

10. Her daughter, Dr Dangledoor, teaches science at a college in Jackson, Miss , where she earned her B A

Commas

Commas are used in dates and addresses, as well as after greetings and closings in a letter.

Add commas where needed to the sentences below. The first one has been done for you.

1. Los Angeles, California, is an exciting city to live in.

2. I moved there on August 20 2000.

3. My aunt lives in Pasadena California.

4. "Dear Jennifer" she wrote, "You would love it here."

5. I used to live in Rochester New York where it would snow.

6. Last year, on December 25 2001 I went to the beach in shorts.

7. "Dear Grandma," I wrote to my grandmother in Albany New York.

8. "Now I know why Aunt Margo loves California. Love Jennifer."

9. Later, I might move down to San Diego California.

10. I'd like to go to college there after I graduate from high school on June 18 2004.

Contractions

A *contraction* is a shortened form of two words combined. An apostrophe takes the place of the missing letter(s).

Rewrite the sentences below, turning the underlined words into contractions. Remember to put the apostrophe in the correct place. The first one has been done for you.

1. <u>We are</u> going to the football game this Saturday. _We're going to the football game this Saturday._

2. <u>We will</u> have to get there early in order to park the car. _____

3. My mother <u>is not</u> going to the game. _____

4. She <u>does not</u> like to see people tackling each other. _____

5. My father says she <u>should not</u> miss this game. _____

6. "<u>It is</u> important," he said. "Whomever wins will go to the Super Bowl." _____

7. "I <u>can not</u> go," Mom said. "<u>I would</u> rather stay home and read." _____

8. Dad and I <u>will not</u> usually miss a game. _____

9. Last week, however, I <u>could not</u> go. _____

10. I was sick in bed, and I <u>was not</u> happy about this. _____

Possessive Nouns

Possessive nouns are those nouns that show belonging. We use an apostrophe to indicate that the noun is possessed by someone or something.

Add apostrophes to the possessive nouns in the sentences below. The first one has been done for you.

1. This is **Amy's** bicycle.

2. She used to ride Georges bike.

3. Sometimes she rode her little sisters skateboard.

4. Her bikes handlebars have tassles on the ends.

5. She likes to ride her bike on her friends farm.

6. The girls ride their bikes on the farms dirt roads.

7. Suzies father waves to them from his tractor.

8. The tractors wheels make huge dirt tracks in the ground.

9. Suzies fathers dog chases the girls on their bikes.

10. Amy is glad to have her own bicycle instead of borrowing her brothers bike or her sisters skateboard.

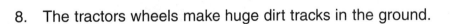

Capital Letters

Capital letters are used to indicate proper nouns, including days of the week, months of the year, street and country names, the names of holidays, and the titles of people.

Rewrite the sentences below, adding capital letters where appropriate. The first one has been done for you.

1. ms. maria blum has always wanted to be a veterinarian. _Ms. Maria Blum has always wanted to be a veterinarian._

2. in january, she started classes at the college in portland, oregon. _____

3. her biology class is taking a field trip to the willamette river in march. _____

4. dr. roberts will ask them to study the birds and plants that live near the river. _____

5. maria is excited to learn about the canadian geese that live there. _____

6. she hopes to travel to canada in june. _____

7. on tuesday, her class will hear a lecture from mr. frank smith. _____

8. mr. smith works at the veterinary clinic on arthur street. _____

9. maria met him at a christmas party the previous december. _____

10. "you'd make a fine veterinarian," he told her. _____

Colons

> **Colons** are placed between hours and minutes when writing times.

Rewrite the following sentences. Add colons where they are needed. The first one has been done for you.

1. The train was supposed to arrive at 945 in the morning. _The train was supposed to arrive at 9:45 in the morning._

2. Angelique looked at her watch at 820. _____

3. She looked again at 900 and realized the train would be late. _____

4. At 1005, the train still hadn't arrived at the station. _____

5. Marty, who had been at the station since 730, grew impatient. _____

6. The stationmaster said the train would arrive at 1015. _____

7. At 1128, the train broke down after it hit a boulder. _____

8. Angelique called Marty at 1145. _____

9. She told him the train wouldn't be fixed until 200 that afternoon. _____

10. He replied that he'd come back at 500 that evening to pick her up. _____

Quotation Marks

Quotation marks appear at the beginning and end of the words a person speaks. Periods, question marks, exclamation points, and commas that are part of the person's speech go inside the quotations. A comma sets off quotations.

Add quotation marks to the sentences below. The first one has been done for you.

1. Marianne woke up and said, "I feel really sick."

2. Maybe you should stay home today, suggested Mother.

3. But I have a book report due! protested Marianne.

4. I am sure your teacher will understand, Mother assured her.

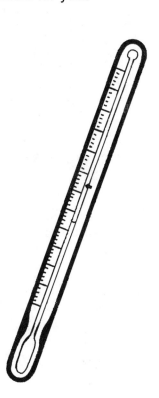

5. Marianne tried to get out of bed, saying, I think I'll be fine.

6. Mother felt her forehead and said, Oh, dear, you have a fever.

7. Stay in bed, and I'll make you some nice, hot soup, said Mother.

8. Will you call my teacher and let her know? Marianne asked.

9. Of course, Mother said. Now I'll go make the soup.

10. It's no fun being sick, said Marianne.

Conjunctions

Conjunctions **link two independent clauses together by using the words** *for, and, nor, but, or, yet,* **and** *so.*

Underline the conjunctions in the sentences below. The first one has been done for you.

1. Vincent van Gogh was a painter, <u>and</u> he was an interesting man.

2. He liked to paint sunflowers, so he spent a lot of time outdoors.

3. He wrote his brother hundreds of letters, for they were very close.

4. His brother Theo wasn't rich, yet he gave Vincent money to keep painting.

5. One of the most famous paintings shows crows in a field, and the picture is full of blues and yellows.

6. Vincent liked to paint with bright colors such as yellow, but he was often depressed.

7. One time, he cut off a piece of his ear, for he was very upset.

8. Vincent didn't sell his paintings during his lifetime, but now they are worth millions.

9. I have not seen his paintings, nor will I get to until next year.

10. Then the local museum will exhibit them, so I will be first in line.

Conjunctions (cont.)

Fill in the blanks with coordinating conjunctions to complete the following sentences. The first one has been done for you.

1. Liddy likes to hike, _____and_____ she likes to identify native plants.

2. She knows many kinds, _____ sometimes she doesn't recognize one.

3. She plucks off one leaf _____ she can take it home and compare it to the pictures in her books.

4. Many native plants can ease aches and pains, _____ you have to use them carefully.

5. You can easily mistake one plant for another, _____ be careful.

6. I like to hike with Liddy, _____ she teaches me many things.

7. For instance, poison oak looks much like blackberries, _____ they are very different.

8. Mugwort takes the itch out of poison oak, _____ I learned to identify it immediately.

9. You can eat miner's lettuce, _____ it doesn't taste like the lettuce you eat in a salad.

10. Liddy dries lavender _____ hangs it in her closet to make her clothes smell nice.

Exclamations

Exclamations are used to show surprise, fear, or other strong emotions.

Underline the exclamations in the sentences below. The first one has been done for you.

1. <u>"Ouch!"</u> Melissa cried as the kitten scratched her hand.

2. "Yikes!" Bobby yelled.

3. "This cat has sharp claws," he added. "Wow!"

4. Melissa cuddled the kitten against her neck. "Help!"

5. "What?" asked Bobby. "Oh!"

6. The kitten leapt onto the dog's back, crying "Meow!"

7. "Look!" said Bobby.

8. "Amazing!" shouted Melissa.

9. The dog looked around at the kitten on his back and said, "Woof!"

10. "Ha!" exclaimed Melissa. "They like each other."

Exclamations *(cont.)*

Fill in the blank spaces in the sentences below with exclamations. The first one has been done for you.

1. _____*"Gee!"*_____ said Ryan when he saw the great-horned owl.

2. The owl spread its wings, and Annie cried, "_____"

3. "_____" warned the teacher, pointing out the owl's sharp talons.

4. Ryan looked at the feathers covering the owl's toes and exclaimed, "_____"

5. "_____" said the owl, blinking at the class.

6. "_____" said the teacher. "Owls eat live mice, snakes, and smaller birds."

7. Annie wrinkled her nose in disgust and cried, "_____"

8. "_____" explained the teacher. "The owl's feathers allow it to fly silently through the forest."

9. Ryan looked into the owl's wise yellow eyes. "_____" he gasped.

10. The teacher gave the owl a worm. "_____" she winced, wiping her hands on a napkin.

Imperatives

Imperatives **are usually requests or commands. The subject is usually implied, rather than stated.**

Underline the imperative in each sentence. The first one has been done for you.

1. "<u>Throw the ball!</u>" yelled the girl on first base.

2. "Catch it!" cried the crowd.

3. The shortstop caught the ball and cried, "Watch out!"

4. Jan threw the ball to the pitcher, who said, "Get ready!"

5. The crowd hollered, "Go back to third!"

6. "Look out!" Misty cried, sliding into third base.

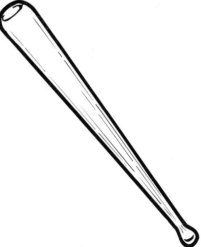

7. "Keep your eye on the ball!" the pitcher said.

8. A new batter walked up to the plate and said, "Pitch a curveball."

9. "Be careful," the coach warned.

10. "Run home!" the crowd called to Misty.

Sentence Structure

A complete sentence contains both a *subject* and a *predicate*. The subject tells who or what the sentence is about. The predicate tells what the subject is doing.

Circle the subject and underline the predicate in the spaces below. The first one has been done for you.

1. (Kevin) pulled the wagon.

2. His baby sister laughed and sang.

3. He trotted like a horse.

4. The baby clapped her hands.

5. A dog walked by the wagon.

6. He stopped to sniff the wheel.

7. The wagon rumbled over rocks.

8. It started to rain.

9. Kevin ran with the wagon.

10. He and his sister arrived home soaking wet.

Sentence Structure *(cont.)*

> A *sentence* contains a subject and a verb. It begins with a capital letter and ends with a period, question mark, or exclamation point.

The sentences below are missing punctuation, capital letters, and in some cases, quotation marks. Punctuate the sentences. The first one has been done for you.

1. I would like to make cookies Mark told his father ___"I would like to make cookies,"___

    ___Mark told his father.___

2. fine Dad said Let's get out the ingredients _____

    _____

3. Mark and Dad took out flour sugar butter and salt _____

    _____

4. they found chocolate chips and walnuts in the pantry _____

    _____

5. Where are the cookie sheets Mark asked Dad _____

    _____

6. dad found the cookie sheets and greased them with butter _____

    _____

7. the dough tasted delicious _____

    _____

8. mark dropped dough onto the cookie sheets and opened the oven door _____

    _____

9. ouch he cried as his hand touched the inside of the oven _____

    _____

10. be careful said Dad we're cooking the cookies, not your hand _____

    _____

Sentence Fragments

Sentence fragments occur when a sentence is missing a subject or verb.

Fix the sentence fragments below by rewriting the sentences with the addition of a subject or verb. The first one has been done for you.

1. Wanted to sew a dress. _Aunt Yumi wanted to sew a dress._
    _____

2. She fabric, a pattern, and thread. _____
    _____

3. pinned the fabric to the pattern and cut it out. _____
    _____

4. was purple with yellow polka dots. _____
    _____

5. said, "This is going to be a beautiful dress!" _____
    _____

6. She it on the sewing machine. _____
    _____

7. The needed buttons in the back. _____
    _____

8. sewed the buttons on with a needle and thread. _____
    _____

9. tried on the dress in front of a mirror. _____
    _____

10. walked in and said, "You look pretty!" _____
    _____

Run-on Sentences

Run-on sentences occur when two sentences containing a subject and a verb run together without any punctuation.

Fix the run-on sentences below by rewriting the sentences with the addition of punctuation and/or other words. The first one has been done for you.

1. Most doctors say that it is important to exercise three times a week this keeps your body physically fit. _Most doctors say that it is important to exercise three times a week. This keeps your body physically fit._

2. You can try running, biking, or swimming all three are good forms of exercise. _____

3. The point is to get your heart rate up for twenty minutes this is called aerobic exercise. _____

4. It is also good to do strength training lifting weights can make you stronger. _____

5. Some people say they don't have time to exercise they should make a few changes. _____

6. You can park your car far away from a store or the office you will get in a good, quick walk this way. _____

7. You can climb the stairs instead of taking the elevator climbing burns calories and keeps you fit. _____

8. Playing on a sports team also provides the body with exercise football, soccer, and rugby keep the players running. _____

9. There are many forms of exercise choose your favorite and get moving! _____

Double Negatives

Double negatives occur when you use two negatives in one sentence.

Rewrite each sentence so that it only contains one negative. The first one has been done for you.

1. I don't like to do no homework. _I don't like to do any homework._

2. Math isn't fun neither. _____

3. Spelling doesn't give me no thrill. _____

4. I don't like no subjects at school. _____

5. Mom says I can't go nowhere until I do my homework. _____

6. I don't want to sit in my room no more. _____

7. I can't get no one to help me. _____

8. My teacher won't like it when I don't turn in no work. _____

9. Dad says I can't talk to no one on the phone until I finish my homework. _____

10. My life isn't no fun. _____

I and Me

The pronouns *I*, *me*, *my*, and *mine* function different ways in different sentences.

Circle the correct word in each sentence below and write it on the corresponding line. The first one has been done for you.

1. Halloween is (**mine,** **my**) favorite holiday.

2. (**I, Me**) like the scary costumes and the candy.

3. (**Mine, My**) costume this year is a witch.

4. Dad made it out of black velvet for (**I, me**).

5. This pumpkin is (**my, mine**).

6. Mother bought pumpkins for Dad and (**I, me**).

7. He and (**I, me**) carved them together.

8. Now (**we, us**) are going trick-or-treating.

9. Dad has a costume like (**my, mine**).

10. He thinks he will get more candy than (**I, me**).

Assessment

Fill in the bubble in front of the correct answer in each group.

1. The gooses flew overhead in a V-shaped formation.

   Ⓐ The gice flew overhead   Ⓒ The geeses flew overhead
   Ⓑ The geese flew overhead   Ⓓ (No Mistakes)

2. Yesterday, we played kickball in the rain.

   Ⓐ Yesterday, we play   Ⓒ Yesterday, we are going to play
   Ⓑ Yesterday, we will play   Ⓓ (No Mistakes)

3. "Ouch?" cried the girl after she touched the cactus.

   Ⓐ "Ouch," cried the girl   Ⓒ "Ouch." Cried the girl.
   Ⓑ "Ouch!" cried the girl   Ⓓ (No Mistakes)

4. Ms Shimmel takes care of injured birds.

   Ⓐ MS Shimmel   Ⓒ Ms. Shimmel
   Ⓑ M.S. Shimmel   Ⓓ (No Mistakes)

5. Her plane is due to arrive at 445 in the afternoon.

   Ⓐ 4:45 in the afternoon   Ⓒ 4.45 in the afternoon
   Ⓑ 44:5 in the afternoon   Ⓓ (No Mistakes)

6. "We don't got no chocolate milk," said Matt.

   Ⓐ "We didn't got no chocolate milk,"   Ⓒ "We don't have no chocolate milk,"
   Ⓑ "We don't have any chocolate milk,"   Ⓓ (No Mistakes)

7. Running down the hill.

   Ⓐ Running down the steep hill.   Ⓒ Josie is running down the hill.
   Ⓑ My father running down the hill. Ⓓ (No Mistakes)

Assessment *(cont.)*

8. You need to clean your room said Mother.

   (A) "You need to clean your room" said Mother.

   (B) You need to clean your room, said Mother.

   (C) "You need to clean your room," said Mother.

   (D) (No Mistakes)

9. Marie lives in paris, France.

   (A) Marie lives in Paris France.

   (B) Marie lives in Paris, France.

   (C) Marie lives in paris, france.

   (D) (No Mistakes)

10. The orange and white cat

    (A) The orange and white cat, Molly

    (B) The orange and white cat with the torn ear

    (C) The orange and white cat likes pancakes.

    (D) (No Mistakes)

11. Spencer's friend has a surfboard.

    (A) Spencers friend

    (B) Spencers' friend

    (C) Spencers's friend

    (D) (No Mistakes)

12. That bowling ball is my.

    (A) That bowling ball is mine.

    (B) That bowling ball is me.

    (C) That bowling ball is I.

    (D) (No mistakes)

13. John loves to ski he also loves to dance.

    (A) John loves to ski, he also loves to dance.

    (B) John loves to ski. he also loves to dance.

    (C) John loves to ski. He also loves to dance.

    (D) (No mistakes)

14. Lydia was born March 2 1970.

    (A) born March 2. 1970

    (B) born March 2, 1970.

    (C) born march 2, 1970.

    (D) (No Mistakes)

Assessment *(cont.)*

15. It's a beautiful day.

    (A) Its a beautiful day.

    (B) Its' a beautiful day.

    (C) It a beautiful day.

    (D) (No mistakes)

16. The horses gallops in the pasture.

    (A) galloped in the pasture.

    (B) galloping in the pasture.

    (C) was galloping in the pasture.

    (D) (No Mistakes)

17. Tomorrow, we have gone to the circus.

    (A) had gone to the circus

    (B) will go to the circus

    (C) be going to the circus

    (D) (No Mistakes)

18. Marcus hasn't got no money.

    (A) hasn't got none money

    (B) doesn't have no money

    (C) hasn't got any money

    (D) (No Mistakes)

19. The teacher gave the apples to Harvey and me.

    (A) Harvey and I

    (B) I and Harvey

    (C) Harvey and mine

    (D) (No Mistakes)

20. "Stop, thief," the man yelled.

    (A) "Stop, thief."

    (B) "Stop, thief!"

    (C) "Stop, thief?"

    (D) (No Mistakes)

21. A bunch of Native Americans performed special buffalo dances.

    (A) A herd of Native Americans

    (B) A tribe of Native Americans

    (C) A flock of Native American

    (D) (No Mistakes)

Assessment (cont.)

22. Her braided her own hair.

    (A) He braided her own hair.
    (B) She braided her own hair.
    (C) Him braided her own hair.
    (D) (No Mistakes)

23. Maria is going to visit her grandmother.

    (A) Maria are going to visit
    (B) Maria hasn't going to visit
    (C) Maria has going to visit
    (D) (No Mistakes)

24. The clown juggles she has a trained dog.

    (A) The clown juggles. she has a trained dog.
    (B) The clown juggles, and she has a trained dog.
    (C) The clown juggles so she has a trained dog.
    (D) (No Mistakes)

25. Francisco ran quick to the bus stop.

    (A) Francisco ran quickly to the bus stop.
    (B) Francisco ran quicker
    (C) Francisco ran more quick
    (D) (No Mistakes)

26. You can eat your lunch at 1130.

    (A) You can eat your lunch at 11.30.
    (B) You can eat your lunch at 11,30.
    (C) You can eat your lunch at 11:30.
    (D) (No Mistakes)

27. "Wasnt the party fun!" exclaimed Mother.

    (A) "Was'nt the party fun!"
    (B) "Wa'snt the party fun!"
    (C) "Wasn't the party fun!"
    (D) (No Mistakes)

28. Russ sanded the desk. Julia painted it

    (A) Russ sand the desk. Julia paint it.
    (B) Russ sanded the desk, Julia painted it.
    (C) Russ sanded the desk Julia painted it.
    (D) (No Mistakes)

29. "Let's go to a movie!" cried George.

    (A) "Let's go to a movie! cried George.

    (B) "Let's go to a movie!" cried George.

    (C) "Let's go to a movie!" Cried George.

    (D) (No Mistakes)

30. My sister and me play softball on the weekends.

    (A) My sister and myself

    (B) My sister and I

    (C) My sister and mine

    (D) (No Mistakes)

31. I have only a dollar but I can still buy orange juice.

    (A) I have only a dollar for I can still buy orange juice.

    (B) I have only a dollar, nor I can still buy orange juice.

    (C) I have only a dollar, but I can still buy orange juice.

    (D) (No Mistakes)

32. The boy waved sad at his departing mother.

    (A) The boy waved saddest at his departing mother.

    (B) The boy waved sadly at his departing mother.

    (C) The boy waved more sad at his departing mother.

    (D) (No Mistakes)

33. Hurrah I cried as Katie crossed the finish line.

    (A) "Hurrah" I cried as Katie crossed the finish line.

    (B) Hurrah! I cried as Katie crossed the finish line.

    (C) "Hurrah!" I cried as Katie crossed the finish line.

    (D) (No Mistakes)

34. The cat, which just gave birth to kittens.

    (A) The cat, which just gave birth to kittens, likes cheese.

    (B) The cat, which just gave birth to kittens, orange and white.

    (C) The cat, which just gave birth to kittens!

    (D) (No Mistakes)

Assessment *(cont.)*

35. george washington was the first American president.

    Ⓐ George washington was the first American president.

    Ⓑ George Washington was the first american president.

    Ⓒ George Washington was the first American president.

    Ⓓ (No Mistakes)

36. Mother sent the sick woman a ton of flowers.

    Ⓐ a bunch of flowers

    Ⓑ a bouquet of flowers

    Ⓒ a herd of flowers

    Ⓓ (No Mistakes)

37. All the child knew the words to "America the Beautiful."

    Ⓐ All the children

    Ⓑ All the childs

    Ⓒ All the children's

    Ⓓ (No Mistakes)

38. Yesterday, we played soccer.

    Ⓐ Yesterday, we play soccer.

    Ⓑ Yesterday, we will play soccer.

    Ⓒ Yesterday, we have played soccer.

    Ⓓ (No Mistakes)

39. Mrs Blume is an excellent writer who lives in the USA.

    Ⓐ Mrs. Blume is an excellent writer who lives in the USA.

    Ⓑ Mrs. Blume is an excellent writer who lives in the .s.a.

    Ⓒ Mrs. Blume is an excellent writer who lives in the U.S.A.

    Ⓓ (No Mistakes)

40. Terrorists attacked the World Trade Center on September 11 2001.

    Ⓐ on September, 11 2001

    Ⓑ on September 11, 2001

    Ⓒ on September 11 2001,

    Ⓓ (No Mistakes)